Session Skills
for Vocals
Initial-Grade 2

 Free downloads

Published by
Trinity College London Press Ltd
trinitycollege.com

Registered in England
Company no. 09726123

Copyright © 2015 Trinity College London
Second impression, May 2019

Printed in England by Caligraving Ltd
Written, recorded and produced by Camden Music Services.
Exercises devised by Jane Watkins, backing tracks by Tom Fleming.

SESSION SKILLS

CONTENTS

SESSION SKILLS

INTRODUCTION

To be a great rock and pop musician you need to develop a range of important musical skills – from performing with flair to improvising and picking up new songs quickly. Trinity College London's Rock & Pop exams are designed to help you develop these skills and take your musicianship to the next level.

An important part of each Rock & Pop exam is the **session skills** test. For this you can choose either **playback** or **improvising**:

- ⚡ **Playback** involves playing some music you have not seen or heard before, testing your ability to pick up new musical material quickly

- ⚡ **Improvising** involves performing an improvisation over a backing track, testing your ability to respond creatively to a specified musical style and chord sequence.

About this book

This book is specially designed to help you prepare for the session skills test at Initial to Grade 2, whether you choose playback or improvising. It contains plenty of example tests to use for practice, and backing tracks can be downloaded free from **soundwise.co.uk** (see inside back cover for details). It also includes specific guidance on how to approach playback and improvising at Initial, Grade 1 and Grade 2.

Please note that Rock & Pop exams require you to perform three songs as well as the session skills test. A range of songs for each grade level are provided in a separate series of Rock & Pop song books, also published by Trinity. Additional songs can be downloaded at **trinityrock.com**, where you can also find the syllabus and a range of resources for teaching and learning. The syllabus can change from time to time, so check the website regularly to make sure you are referring to an up-to-date version.

SESSION SKILLS

THE TESTS

Playback

If you choose playback for the session skills test, you'll be asked to perform some music you have not seen or heard before. You'll be given a song chart and 30 seconds to study it and try out any sections. The examiner will then play the backing track.

You should listen to the backing track, singing back what you hear and reading the music from the song chart if you want. You'll hear a series of short melodic phrases – you should repeat each of these straight back in turn. A count-in will be given at the beginning of the backing track, and a backing rhythm will play throughout.

In the exam you'll have two chances to sing along with the backing track: first time for practice and second time for assessment. If you choose to read the music from the song chart, remember that for each repeated phrase you should listen the first time and sing the second time.

Improvising

If you choose improvising for the session skills test, you'll be asked to improvise in a specific style over a backing track you have not heard before. You'll be given a chord chart, and the examiner will play a short section of the backing track to give you a feel for the tempo and style. You'll have 30 seconds to study the chord chart and try out any sections. The examiner will then play the backing track.

You should improvise in the specified style over the backing track, which will consist of four repetitions of the chord sequence shown on the chord chart. A count-in will be given at the beginning of the backing track, and a backing rhythm will play throughout.

In the exam you'll have two chances to sing along with the backing track: first time for practice and second time for assessment. A count-in will be given both times.

SESSION SKILLS

PARAMETERS

Trinity provides a full set of parameters for the session skills tests. Published online at **trinityrock.com**, these tell you which musical elements are featured in improvising and playback at each grade. All the example tests in this book have been written to fit with these parameters, so you can be sure that the test in the exam will be similar to the examples in this book.

The following is a summary of the parameters for Initial to Grade 2. Visit **trinityrock.com** for the full set of parameters across all grades.

Playback

For vocalists at Initial to Grade 2, playback is always eight bars long. Within this, each phrase is two bars long, making a total of four phrases. At Initial the time signature is always $\frac{4}{4}$ and at Grade 1 it can be either $\frac{4}{4}$ or $\frac{2}{4}$. At Grade 2 it can be $\frac{4}{4}$, $\frac{2}{4}$ or $\frac{3}{4}$.

You can expect to see minims (half notes) and crotchets (quarter notes) in playback at Initial, with no rests. At Grade 1 semibreves (whole notes) and quavers (eight notes) can also appear, as well as crotchet rests. At Grade 2 there can also be dotted minims and ties.

No dynamics feature at Initial, but $\boldsymbol{p}$ and $\boldsymbol{f}$ are used at Grade 1 and 2, so to try to observe these dynamics where they appear. At Initial the key is either C major or A minor, with G major and E minor also appearing at Grade 1, and F major and D minor appearing at Grade 2.

The melody only features stepwise movement at Initial, with larger intervals between notes appearing at Grades 1 and 2: major/minor 3rds at Grade 1, and perfect 4ths at Grade 2. The overall melodic range is a 4th at Initial and a 6th at Grades 1 and 2.

Improvising

For vocalists at Initial to Grade 2, the chord sequence is always four bars long with one chord per bar. The backing track consists of four repetitions of this sequence, requiring an improvisation that lasts 16 bars in total. The time signature is always $\frac{4}{4}$ at Initial and Grade 1. At Grade 2 it can also be $\frac{3}{4}$.

At Initial the chord sequence can be in any major key, and at Grades 1 and 2 it can be in any major or minor key. Chords I, IV and V are mainly featured at Initial, with chords on any degree of the scale (simple major and minor chords only) introduced at Grade 1 and Grade 2.

Improvising at Initial is in either simple rock or pop style. At Grade 1 it can also be in ballad or heavy rock style, with country style appearing at Grade 2.

INITIAL PLAYBACK

Example 1

Example 2

Example 3

Example 4

TOP TIP Remember that to perform the playback test you can read from the song chart or copy what you hear by listening to the backing track – or both. It's up to you and there is no right or wrong way of doing it.

Example 5

Example 6

Example 7

Example 8

Example 9

Example 10

INITIAL IMPROVISING

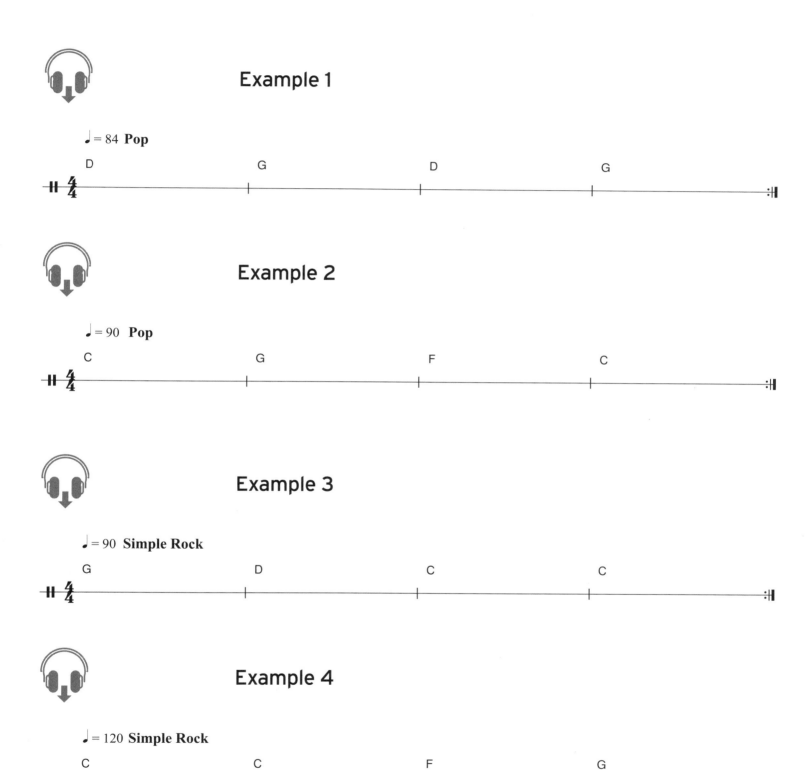

Example 1

♩ = 84 **Pop**

D	G	D	G

Example 2

♩ = 90 **Pop**

C	G	F	C

Example 3

♩ = 90 **Simple Rock**

G	D	C	C

Example 4

♩ = 120 **Simple Rock**

C	C	F	G

Example 5

♩ = 80 **Pop**

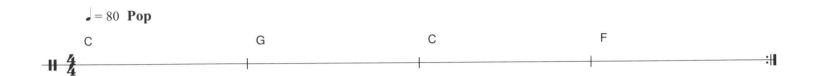

C   G   C   F

TOP TIP   Remember that you can use any appropriate vowel sound to perform both improvising and playback – for example 'la' or 'do'.

Example 6

♩ = 84 **Pop**

G   C   D   D

Example 7

♩ = 90 **Simple Rock**

D   A   A   G

Example 8

♩ = 100 **Simple Rock**

| C | F | F | G |

Example 9

♩ = 80 **Pop**

| D | G | G | A |

TOP TIP You don't have to fill your whole improvisation with notes – remember that you can also use rests, or silences. Can you practise using rests in your improvisations to make some effective contrasts with the notes?

Example 10

♩ = 90 **Simple Rock**

| G | D | D | G |

GRADE 1 PLAYBACK

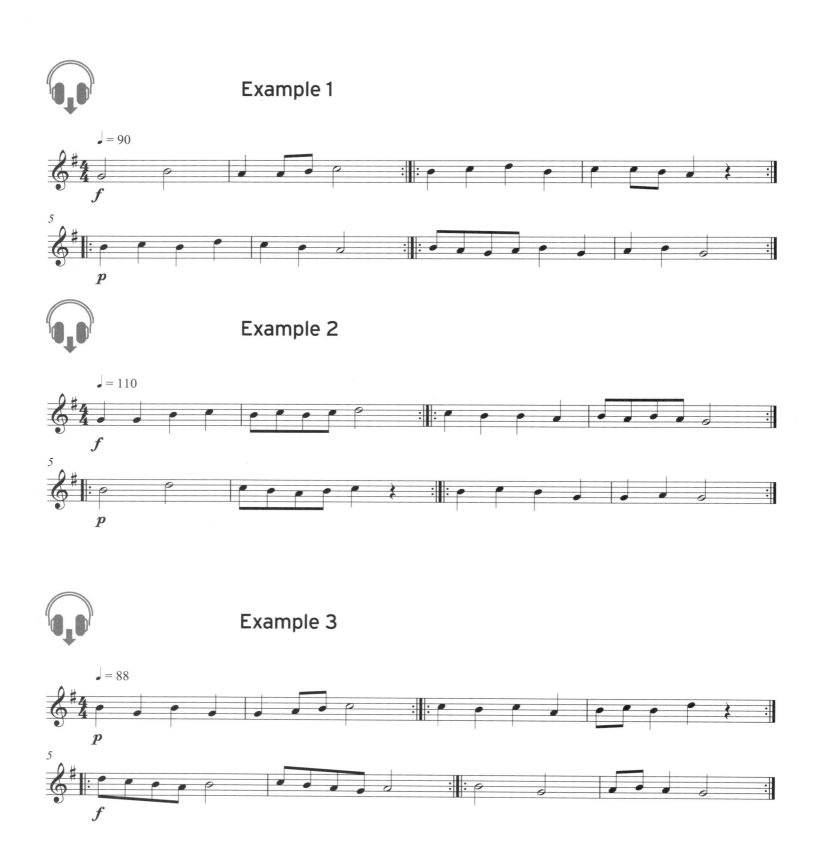

Example 1

Example 2

Example 3

Example 4

TOP TIP Notice that quavers (eighth notes) are featured in the playback test at Grade 1. Listen carefully to the backing track to help you sing these in time with the beat.

Example 5

Example 6

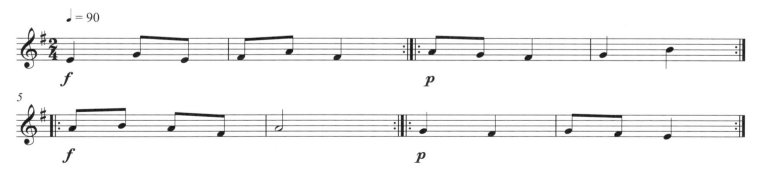

Example 7

Example 8

Example 9

Example 10

GRADE 1 IMPROVISING

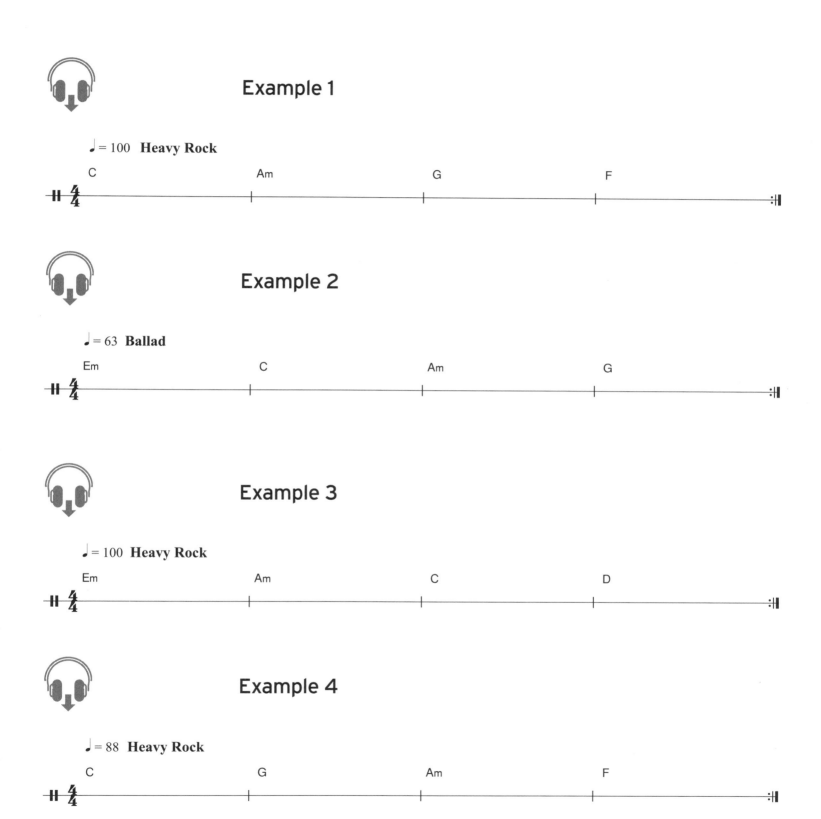

Example 1

♩ = 100 **Heavy Rock**

| C | Am | G | F |

Example 2

♩ = 63 **Ballad**

| Em | C | Am | G |

Example 3

♩ = 100 **Heavy Rock**

| Em | Am | C | D |

Example 4

♩ = 88 **Heavy Rock**

| C | G | Am | F |

Example 5

♩ = 96 **Pop**

| D | G | Em | A |

TOP TIP Notice that a different chord symbol is written above each bar, showing you that each bar has a different harmonic foundation. When you sing, listen for these changes and try to find notes that sound good with the chord in each bar.

Example 6

♩ = 70 **Ballad**

| Dm | B♭ | Gm | A |

Example 7

♩ = 96 **Heavy Rock**

| Am | G | Dm | Em |

Example 8

♩ = 72 **Ballad**

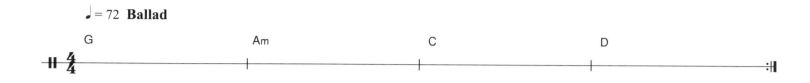

| G | Am | C | D |

Example 9

♩ = 70 **Ballad**

| D | Em | Bm | G |

TOP TIP The word at the top of each example describes its style. You should try to capture this in your improvisation, so listen to a range of music to become familiar with the different styles. A good way to start is by searching for different styles online.

Example 10

♩ = 108 **Simple Rock**

| Gm | D | Gm | Cm |

GRADE 2 PLAYBACK

Example 1

Example 2

Example 3

Example 4

TOP TIP Notice that ties are used in playback at Grade 2, creating a syncopated or off-beat effect. Listen carefully to the rhythms that feature ties to help you capture these rhythms when you perform them.

Example 5

Example 6

Example 7

Example 8

Example 9

Example 10

GRADE 2 IMPROVISING

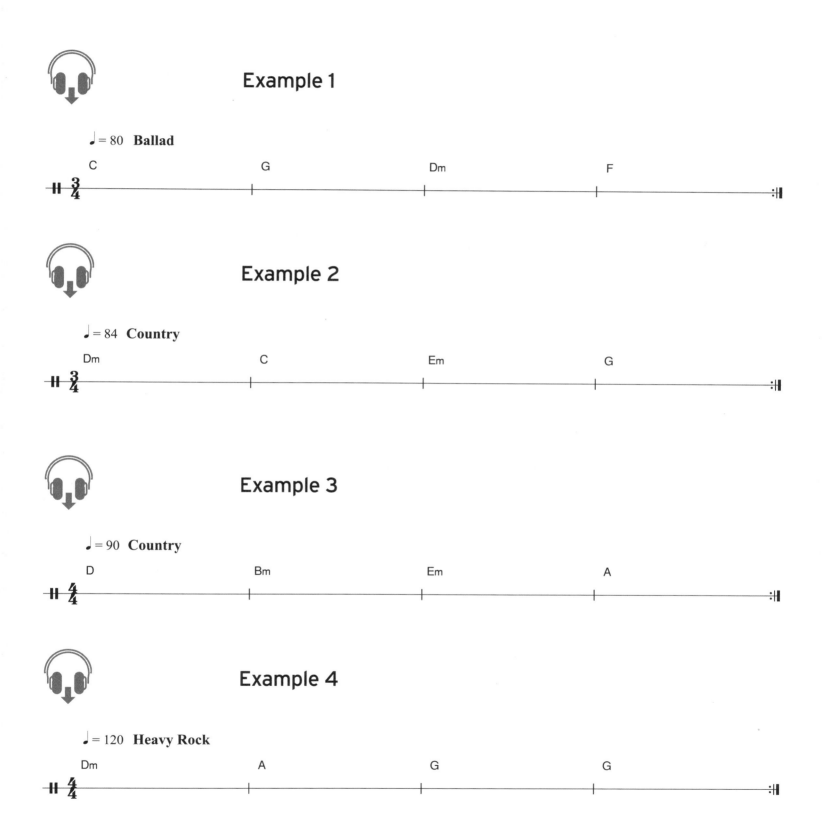

Example 1

♩ = 80 **Ballad**

C	G	Dm	F

Example 2

♩ = 84 **Country**

Dm	C	Em	G

Example 3

♩ = 90 **Country**

D	Bm	Em	A

Example 4

♩ = 120 **Heavy Rock**

Dm	A	G	G

Example 5

♩ = 96 **Simple Rock**

 F   Dm   Gm   C

> **TOP TIP** Listen online to other musicians improvising and think about what makes a good improvisation. Are the best improvisations complex, or can good improvising also be very simple?

Example 6

♩ = 82 **Ballad**

Dm   Am   G   Dm

Example 7

♩ = 92 **Country**

Bm   Em   G   A

Example 8

♩ = 104 **Simple Rock**

| G | C | Em | D |

Example 9

♩ = 100 **Country**

| Dm | G | Em | A |

 **TOP TIP** If you are familiar with sol-fa then it's fine to use this in your improvisation if you want to. Otherwise you can use any appropriate vowel sound.

Example 10

♩ = 96 **Country**

| F | C | Gm | B♭ |